D0783509

The Frustrated Commuter's Companion

The Frustrated Commuter's Companion

You might be late, but you are not alone

Jonathan Swan

For Katharine, who loves staying home

1 3 5 7 9 10 8 6 4 2

Pop Press, an imprint of Ebury Publishing,
20 Vauxhall Bridge Road,
London SW1V 2SA

Pop Press is part of the Penguin Random House group
of companies whose addresses can be found at
global.penguinrandomhouse.com

Copyright © Pop Press 2017

First published by Pop Press in 2017

www.penguin.co.uk

A CIP catalogue record for this book is available
from the British Library

ISBN 9781785037474

Printed and bound in Great Britain by Clays Ltd, St Ives PLC

Penguin Random House is committed to a sustainable future
for our business, our readers and our planet. This book is made
from Forest Stewardship Council® certified paper.

Road rage, air rage. Why should I be forced to divide my rage into separate categories? To me, it's just one big, all-around, everyday rage. I don't have time for fine distinctions. I'm busy screaming at people

George Carlin

COMMUTER COMRADES!

It is time for us to revolt! Or, if not revolt, to write a very strongly worded email to the chief executives of the railways. We must take to the streets and demonstrate! (Although we will have to start after the morning rush to let the traffic die down a bit.)

For too long we have been treated as second-class citizens, even though we have seen there are empty seats in first class. We have waited patiently at the bus stop, only to be pushed aside by school kids who don't queue and get in through the back doors, which we all know are for getting off only. We have stood on the tube platforms when train after train passes with no room for us to board.

It is time for us to fight back. Hear us tut and tremble, Southern Rail, for we are disgruntled. If you are in charge – beware! We are coming for you. (Even if it is on a rail replacement bus service. We will remember to add extra time for our journey.) We are not going to stand for this any longer; we've stood for long enough, all the way from Birmingham to Euston.

Our good manners and horror of confrontation have kept us, and before us, our fathers, and their fathers before them, quiet for too long. But now we've had one backpack swung in our faces on a crowded train too many. Our demands are simple. Roads that flow freely, with all white vans and parents on the morning school run banned. No cancelled trains, and a full public naming and shaming for the drivers of late running trains. Buses that don't travel in packs of three.

This book is a call to arms and a beacon of solidarity amongst commuters. Whenever you see a fellow traveller with a copy, give them the secret sign of the commuter: ignore them completely, even though your lips are closer to theirs than they usually are to those of your beloved. But inside you both will know that you are part of a silent army.

We are legion. We are commuters. We are coming. But we will probably be at least half an hour late.

The Obstacle

Related to the genus *phonus idioticus*, with the ability to completely ignore all outside stimuli apart from whatever is on its phone screen, *The Obstacle* is known for stopping abruptly wherever is most inconvenient for its fellow commuters. It can often be found at the entrance and exit of platforms, and, most confusingly, stock-still at the bottom of escalators, where it is able to cause mass pile-ups with its unpredictable behaviour.

Comfort paradox (n.)

The *comfort paradox* applies mostly to rail commuters. The paradox lies in the lengths to which passengers will go to make their commute just a tiny bit better, no matter how ridiculous. It is based on the misguided idea that you can somehow beat the system; that there exists a 'better way'. A classic comfort paradox is dragging yourself out of bed an hour earlier than you need to so that you can drive to a station nearer the start of the line to be sure of getting a seat, or going to the office on a Sunday to drop off all your work clothes for the week rather than carry them on your bike each day.

Missing word round

The old excuses about the wrong type of rain and leaves on the line are still used all too frequently by train companies. However, sometimes the reason for the hold-up is a little more … unusual. See if you can put the correct missing word into these all-too-real scenarios:

Burglar
Giant clown
Swan
Pikachu
Wallaby

Southeastern: 'We regret to inform you that trains via Charlton are cancelled due to a _____ in a tree'

First Great Western: 'The late running of the train from London Paddington to Cardiff Central is caused by a _____ on the line'

Transport for London: 'We apologise for yesterday's power failure. This was caused by someone capturing the station's _____'

Southwest Trains: 'The delay on the Waterloo–Reading line is being caused by a _____ on the line, who is refusing to move'

TransPennine Express: The 10.33 Manchester Airport to Middlesbrough service will be delayed while we try to capture a _____'

ANSWERS:
- In 2014, trains were cancelled for 17 hours while police talked down a suspected burglar who had climbed a tree overhanging a railway line near Charlton station
- a McDonald's lost their Ronald when the inflatable clown was blown from the roof and onto nearby railway tracks
- A game of Pokemon Go! got a little out of hand at Dalston station in London in 2016
- In 2016, a swan was seen perched on the line near Staines. Services were suspended while rail staff waited for the bird to move
- An escaped wallaby was spotted on the tracks between Huddersfield and Stalybridge and trains were held until the animal hopped off

The rail commuter's serenity prayer no.1

God: Grant me the Serenity to remember what the doctor said about my elevated blood pressure, and accept that there is nothing I can do about the train being late; the Courage to text my boss that I'll be late again for the third time this week; and the Wisdom to not get my hopes up that it will be any different tomorrow.

You have your own company, your own temperature control, your own music – and you don't have to put up with dreadful human beings sitting alongside you

Minister for Public Transport, Steven Norris
on why people prefer to commute by private car

The politics of commuting

Smash the system! Did you realise commuting is a political activity? Every commuter has their own ideology, even if they don't think of themselves as a politics person. What sort of system do you instinctively feel most comfortable with? Warning: you might be more radical than you expect!

Socialism. Fair shares for the common man! Who could disagree? No more first-class carriages sitting half-empty whilst we're all crammed into pleb class like cattle. Equal treatment for all passengers. Potential downside: if you commute by car, you will be forced to carshare and provide free lifts for your fellow proles.

Anarchism. At first glance, anarchy is not a good match with commuting. After all, anarchy seems to be the way that Southern have approached managing their railway and look where that has got us. But on closer examination, maybe there are upsides. After all, in an anarchic system everyone gets a chance to be leader. Surely we could do a better job than the current mob of incompetent fat cats.

Liberalism. Live and let live! Freedom for the individual to do what they want. This all sounds great until you apply it to commuting, where one of the great problems is precisely people expressing their free will and doing what they want. From feet on the seats, to leaking tinny beats from their crappy headphones, these are all reasons why liberalism and commuting don't mix. STAND ON THE LEFT, damn it.

Conservatism. Conservatives look back to a golden age, where steam trains reliably chugged away and buses had chirpy conductors who would no doubt clip the ear of today's misbehaving teenagers. Lovely! So why don't we go back to those golden days? Well, you can't, as it was the Conservatives who decided flogging off the railways and bus companies was a good idea, landing us with the joys of ever-increasing prices coupled with ever-worsening service.

Fascism. Technically speaking, Fascism was great for transport, as it was credited with getting the trains running on time in 1930s Italy, and we all know who built the German motorways … However, as it's also an extreme right-wing and authoritarian system that resulted in the death of millions in the twentieth century, it might be best to give it a miss.

🎧 The commuter's playlist

National Express – The Divine Comedy

Road Rage – Catatonia

From Rush Hour with Love – Republica

The Passenger – Iggy Pop

Crosstown Traffic – Jimi Hendrix

Going Underground – The Clash

The Day We Caught the Train – Ocean Colour Scene

Drive – The Cars

Take the A-Train – Duke Ellington

Road to Hell – Chris Rea

A13 – Billy Bragg

Stuck in a Moment You Can't Get Out of – U2

We Gotta Get Out of This Place – The Animals

Complaint template no.1

Dear _____

I see the road works at the junction of the *A105* and *Acacia Avenue* [insert your own roadworks here] have been going on for 10 weeks now. I use the term 'works' ironically, because no one has seen any work going on here since they put the cones up blocking half the road. I can only assume that the tiny hole you did manage to dig has uncovered some sort of ancient artefact so incalculably important that you are awaiting Tony Robinson to come and tell you what to do. Do please let me know what you have discovered in your 'excavation'. I and the other drivers who sit here for 30 minutes each morning are desperate to know what it could be.

Yours, etc

Please be seated
10 dubious ways to get a seat

Getting a seat is the holy grail for the commuter, but for this you'll need luck and cunning. Put your morals to one side and try these subterfuges to blag a perch.

1. Pretend you're expecting by stealing a 'baby on board' badge from a real pregnant lady. (Note that this is a harder blag for men to pull off.)
2. Nab a crutch from your local infirmary and become strategically lame when you board the bus, guilting someone into giving up their seat.
3. Eschew washing and tending to matters of hygiene for a good few days. Miraculously, seats will appear as people scramble to get away from you.
4. Take your dog, get him a yellow harness, slip on your shades and let people assume you're visually impaired and not just extremely hungover. Note that your pooch must be well enough behaved to fake it as a guide dog – if he's a dim-witted, tail-chasing lummox this scam won't work.
5. Invest in a high-vis vest and a peaked cap. Announce you are doing a ticket inspection. Almost immediately seats will become vacant as fare-dodgers scarper off the train.

6. Embrace your non-conformist side and go for the full eccentric look. Dress like a practising Druid and then carefully watch to see who looks the most mortified. Move straight to this person and stand oppressively close to their seat until they wilt and leave.

7. Exploit the confusion of the train seating system. Insist that someone is sitting in your reserved seat. Chances are that they will be filled with doubt – maybe they *are* in the wrong place. Keen to avoid confrontation or a scene they will soon move.

8. Find a quiet corner before boarding and paint red spots all over your face. Looking like you have some sort of nasty infection will soon clear a space for you. For a really hardened crowd, try gluing bits of desiccated sweetcorn to your skin for that pustulant plague vibe.

9. Channel your inner schoolboy by stocking up on stink bombs, fake puddles of puke and plastic dog turds. Surreptitiously deploy these weapons in a stealthy campaign to drive people from their seats.

10. Beat them at their own game and bring your own seat. A nice folding deckchair plonked down in the middle of a crowded carriage makes a perfect place to while away the journey.

The Gourmand

Most commonly sighted in the mornings and late at night, its offensive aroma gives it away. Travellers are alerted to its presence when a foul reek drenches the bus or train. This, then, is the gourmet commuter, whose unique and uncouth digestive system is able to tolerate a Burger King meal at 8 am in the morning. Its displays of indignation and irritation if the bus hits a bump and it spills food all over itself can provide amusement to the observer, and is a sight that cheers up many who see it.

Please do not make eye contact

Trekking through the Amazon pales into insignificance beside the train journey from Dorset to London. It was the worst journey I've ever done

John Blashford-Snell, explorer

Commuter keep fit

Getting enough exercise can be tricky for the harried commuter, especially when coupled with a diet of unhealthy station food and coffee on the go. Throw in the stress of the daily grind to and from work, and is it any wonder that so many commuters look perpetually grey and slightly sweaty. Fortunately, help is at hand with these simple restorative exercises that any traveller should be able to incorporate into their daily routine.

The 'where's my carriage?' 100 metre sprint

Enliven your journey by occasionally booking a seat on the train. Then enjoy an invigorating sprint along the platform as your allotted carriage whizzes past you to come to a halt at the far end of the station. Can you make it before the doors close? Ignore that chest pain, and feel the burn!

Work your core

You certainly can be beach body ready with this core workout. Irrespective of whether there is a seat available on your train or not, plant your feet

→

firmly shoulder width apart at 45-degrees to the direction of travel. Now surf the train, attempting to stay upright no matter how sharp the cornering. Be prepared to get to know your fellow passengers fairly well as you inevitably land in their laps. Think you've mastered it? Next step, a Virgin Pendolino.

Bus-stop bustle

Not a dance that your grandparents did back in the day whilst awaiting their charabanc, rather a full contact sport for those who like to spice up their daily journey with a bit of low level violence. The rules are simple: at rush hour, competitors rendezvous at the bus stop. The game commences as soon as the bus hoves into view. Preliminary jostling escalates into full scale 'bustling' as the bus stops and competitors all attempt to be first on board. The rules are complex: elderly and frail people are exempt, and those with prams may mount a legitimate charge through the pack. Once these wildcards are out of the way, however, anything goes.

The joy of commuting means that you will often bustle with the same people at the same bus stop every morning. This means that there is a chance to develop a one-on-one personal beef with a fellow commuter. What better way to add some excitement to your day that to cultivate an arch enemy whom you must defeat daily by getting onto the number 43 in front of them. To victory!

Crobics

Invented in New York and quite possibly the inspiration for the opening scene of *LaLa Land*, this is any kind of dance routine that can be carried out in a car. The YMCA, the Macarena or other such party dances are apparently acceptable for Crobics. Unlike elsewhere.

If ...

(With apologies to Rudyard Kipling)

IF you stand on the same platform every day
And yet still believe that the train will arrive on time,
If you can watch every year as ticket prices rise
Way faster than your wages,
Even though the services actually seem to be
    getting worse
The more you have to pay,
If you are fairly sure the train has seats
But you've never actually seen one.

If you have looked upon empty first-class carriages
Whilst the only place for your journey is standing
    in the toilet vestibule
But still been forbidden entry by the guard,
If buses crammed with jeering schoolkids
Sail past your stop every morning,
If teenage backpackers knock your coffee out of
    your hand
And all over your suit and fail to notice
If it's always the up escalator that is broken.

If you can ignore the ominous liquid slopping on
    the floor of the tube
Preferring to let it seep into your shoes than get off
    and be late again,
If you can ignore the drunk bloke sleeping in the seat
With no trousers on
Like all the other passengers are doing,
If you can remain stoical when the train is delayed
And laugh when the bus is cancelled, or the traffic
    snarls up again,
Then you are commuter, my friend.

Priority seat

Please give up this seat
for the severely hungover

Complaint template no.2

Dear _____

So the *8.10 from Dorking* [insert your own train here] was late again. In fact, it's late every day. Having had ample time to consider this problem, I have a solution. Why don't you call it the 8.30 instead, which is when it usually rolls in? Then we'd all know where we stand, wouldn't we? In fact, why don't you move ALL your train times back by 20 minutes or so, to reflect when they roughly arrive.

You're welcome.

Where's my train?

Because it has to be somewhere …

N	T	N	N	T	I	A	A	A
T	I	R	A	T	R	R	I	I
R	N	N	T	R	T	I	T	N
A	I	A	A	R	N	T	N	T
T	R	I	N	T	A	T	I	A
A	I	T	R	T	R	I	R	N
N	R	N	R	N	T	A	I	N
A	T	I	I	N	T	N	I	I
N	R	R	A	T	R	A	T	N

Room for one more?

Think your commuter train is overcrowded? You don't know how good you've got it. Compared with other countries, you are merely mildly inconvenienced. If you really want to see properly crowded trains, take a look at rush hour trains in Japan, where they have, in the past, had to employ 'pushers' to cram as many people as they can into carriages. Called *oshiya,* these uniformed guards had the job of inserting passengers into already packed carriages by manhandling them through the doors. At one point during the 1970s, carriages were running at 221 per cent of their intended capacity. By comparison, the busiest commuter routes in and out of London run at about 148 per cent of capacity.

Irked or incandescent?

Racing heart? Clenched jaw? Red spots in front of your eyes? Yes, of course you're angry, you're a commuter! But to find out just how angry, choose from this list of just deserts for transport bosses.

The fat cats who profit from commuters' misery should:

a) Be made to travel all day, every day, on their own train services for one year
b) Be named and shamed on the back of milk bottles as dangerous criminals
c) Have all their pay confiscated and redistributed to season ticket holders
d) Be available at the station, in stocks with large amounts of rotten veg alongside, so they can personally explain why the service is late or cancelled

Bus drivers who drive past your stop without stopping should:

a) Be given glasses so they can recognise a bus stop when one comes up

b) Be made to personally give a piggyback to work to every passenger they ignored

c) Be forced to ride upstairs at the back of the bus in the middle of a pack of teenagers all playing tinny gangsta rap from their phones at once

d) Have to drive a night bus every Friday, Saturday and New Year's Eve

Road bosses who start minor roadworks that last for months should:

a) Be made to dance a jig by the side of the road with a traffic cone on their head

b) Be made to do all the excavations by hand with a teaspoon

c) Be made to wash all the waiting cars whilst they are queueing at the temporary lights

d) Be buried alive in the roadworks

Drivers who park in the cycle lane should:

a) Have their car removed and crushed before their eyes

b) Be forced to travel everywhere on a bike with no saddle for one year

c) Be made to run alongside cyclists and give them a helping push up hills

d) Be sentenced to life in a chain gang hand-painting new bike lanes

→

You answered:

Mostly a or b. Good news. Your humanity hasn't completely been worn away yet. Keep up the good work, and maintain that glimmer of perspective you have retained against the odds

Mostly c. Critical. You might still be saved, but you need to think about getting out of the commute before you become a monster

Mostly d. Oh dear. You are the avenging angel of commuters, bringer of wrath and righteous justice. A coronary check-up is recommended

Londoners are apologetic about their underground, which they believe has become filthy and noisy and dangerous, but which is in fact far more civilised than the average American wedding reception

Dave Berry

The pantomime dame (n.)

There is nothing like the uncomfortable jolt when you spot a work colleague on the train. What is the correct etiquette? This scenario calls for the move known as the *pantomime dame*, where you studiously ignore the obvious: 'he's behind you!'. Play dumb, look the other way or stare at your newspaper so as not to catch their eye. After all, chances are that they saw you first and are pulling the same move. Of course, if your eyes meet then you must acknowledge each other, but, in this case, a nod of greeting is sufficient.

A problem remains, though. You colleague will no doubt be getting off at the same stop as you and walking to the office. To avoid getting stuck with them, you need the classic drag and drop move, where you drag your heels, getting off at the last possible second, and then drop to the back of the queue to leave the station. Keep them in sight and maintain a distance of at least 15 metres at all times.

Between 07:00–09:00 and
17:00–19:00 this station will be
hugely overcrowded. Please try
not to fall onto the tracks.

What they say and what they mean no.1

Buffet car

An area of the train set aside for passengers to purchase food and drink. In the olden days, this would have been a spread of tantalizing foods arranged on a crisp, white-clothed table, possibly brought to you by an efficient and deferential waiter. Nowadays of course it's a sad selection of oily pasties, crisps and weak tea. Mysteriously, most sandwiches come lukewarm in a foil bag and are called a 'melt'.

Express service

Marketed by the train or bus company as a more efficient, direct service that will get you where you need to go the fastest way possible. In reality, your 'express' bus or train will pull in between two and four minutes in front of the non-express one, at double the cost.

Ticket machine

Found at railway stations, they are ostensibly there to receive money and dispense tickets. In fact, they are labyrinthine systems designed to confuse even Alan Turing. What sort of return do you want? Off peak? On peak? Are you going via Hull? Will you be using HS2, travelling with a pogo stick or wearing a hat? You then end up with a ticket that may or may not be valid for your journey, that costs three times more than when you looked it up online yesterday.

The Party Animal

Recognisable by its oscillating pupils, slightly sweaty face and a distinctive musk of booze, *The Party Animal* is often found grimly swaying on the bus in yesterday's clothes. Although its short-term memory is often shot to pieces, it is driven by a primal instinct that says it must get to work by 9 am, although it probably can't exactly tell you why. If pushed on this, it may tell you that it has to earn back all the money blown the night before. Interestingly, *The Party Animal* can often be seen going the opposite way on the bus at about 9.30 am after the boss has taken one look at it and sent it home.

☹ Depressing commuter fact no.1

It never gets better

Commuting newbies might console themselves with the idea that, although it's awful, they'll get habituated to it and it won't seem so bad in a few months. But hard-bitten veterans can derive some cruel pleasure by shooting this fanciful notion down: you never get used to it, and there's science that can prove it. A Harvard University psychologist found that people just can't adapt to commuting, because it's so unpredictable. Looking desperately for a bright side, the hell of commuting might be soul-destroying, but at least it's got variety.

Late again?

Use this handy excuse builder

A	B	C
So sorry	Prince Philip	Stole my wallet
You won't believe this	My dog	Died
I know I'm late again but	I thought	It was the weekend
I can't believe it	By mistake	Went to my old job
Realised too late	A pregnant woman	Was wearing my wife's high heels

Forget the tired old bus/train was late, or stuck in traffic excuses. Get creative by choosing one each from column A, B and C to generate your own unique excuses.

A	B	C
Just as I left	Aliens	Hid my car keys
Have you heard	Janet from Accounts	Had a baby on the bus
It sounds crazy	The bus driver	Drove the wrong way
Apologies	My alarm	Was sick on my trousers
I don't understand it	My mum	Failed to wake me

How much?

The average price of a train season ticket in the UK is £2,493. That's about 10 per cent of an ordinary person's salary, or to put it another away, it's worth about five weeks of your wages every year, just to pay for the pleasure of getting to work! Surely there are better things to spend it on? So what else could you get for the two-and-a-half grand you are forking out to your train company?

- Buy 714 bacon butties at the station

- Hire a chauffeur-driven limo to whisk you to work for a fortnight in style

- Engage a butler for a couple of weeks to *Downton* up your life. They can smooth your morning routine, and greet you with a cocktail when you get home at night

- Go and live for five years in Bhutan, a country where the government ranks happiness as the most important national statistic

- Charter a helicopter, and arrive at work like a head of state

- Bring your packed lunch to work in a Gucci Dionysus handbag

- Buy 1,000 cappuccinos from Starbucks

- Buy 1,700 shares in the rail company, so at least you might make some money back to compensate for your daily misery

… and if you add it all up, the money you spend on commuting would, over the course of your working life, experts reckon, be enough to buy you a house on the paradise island of Bali!

You never really
learn to swear until
you learn to drive

Steven Wright

Commuting survival tips

Getting to and from work is dangerous. Memorise these tips, and let's stay safe out there today people!

On the train

Understand how the toilet door works. You DO NOT want the door sliding open to reveal you sat with pants round ankles to the crowded carriage as you rattle through Northampton. The safest approach is to take care of business before you board.

Remember: you snooze, you lose. There is nothing sorrier than a commuter who has dozed off, missed their stop and finds themselves stuck in some far-flung terminus miles past home. Consider packing a small chalkboard so you can alert fellow commuters to your intended destination. They will almost certainly ignore this, but you can try.

In the car

You are not invisible. However at home you feel in the warm cocoon of the driver's seat, remember other people can see you. If you're rooting around in your nostrils when you're stuck in heavy traffic, expect to find a coach-load of teens in the next lane laughing and taking pictures of you.

Stick to your route. However tempted you are to escape the jams and find a new way, resist it. You'll only end up getting lost and be even later for work. Remember, Christopher Columbus discovered America whilst he was looking for India. Who knows where you'll end up?

On the bus

The morning bus is the domain of youngsters on their way to school. You are only a visitor to their world. Remain apart and aloof. Under no circumstances do anything to attract attention to yourself: this is not a time to try to ingratiate yourself by trying out your street talk, fam. The resulting mockery will be so fierce that you will be transported instantly back to your teen self, burning with embarrassment as the cool kids laugh at your shoes and flick your ears.

Bonus tip: Don't stand in the bit of the bus reserved for parents with buggies. They don't like it, and will let you know. If it's really crowded, don't suggest they fold up their pushchair. Let the driver do this – at least he's got the glass screen to protect him.

Cycling

Don't go too close to parked cars. Don't go too near the middle of the road. Don't go on the pavement. Don't ride on wet drain covers. Don't go round lorries or buses. Don't give drivers the finger. Don't take on taxi drivers. Don't ride with headphones on. Don't assume pedestrians won't suddenly leap out in front of you. In fact, just don't.

Commuter's lexicon

Non-stop roulette (n.)

An occasional game of chance, compulsorily inflicted on unwilling commuters. *Non-stop roulette* begins when it is announced that the train you are on will no longer be calling at your station, due to some incompetence by the train operator. The 'fun' in the game lies in trying to find out where the damn train will actually stop and let you off, and how you will get back home from there. Watch seasoned commuters as they mentally scroll through every possible alternative route and connection, like Rain Man counting cards.

Public transportation is for jerks and lesbians

Homer Simpson

Anger management

Getting angry and commuting go together like winter and the wrong kind of rain. But the red mist takes people in different ways. Are you Simmering from Salford, or Exasperated from Exeter?

The sigher

This traveller greets setbacks with a sigh of resignation. They are *disappointed* with the train company in much the same way they are *disappointed* to find their children smoking behind the shed with the naughty boy from next door. They pride themselves on their common-sense attitude, and consider a stiff upper lip as at least as important as the ability to read and write.

The tutter

The tutter likes other people to know that they are cross. A conformist at heart, the tutter likes nothing better than the ripple of clucks that occurs when lots of people tut in unison when bad news is announced. In times of stress this herd clucking helps reassure them that they are amongst their own kind.

The twitcher

Highly strung, this commuter's circuit board is dangerously overloaded. Every delay, late-running service or cancellation sends a dangerous power surge through their system, eliciting flinches and tics of suppressed frustration. Other passengers stay clear, sensing that the twitcher could fatally short circuit at any minute.

The Krakatoa

Like the volcano, this passenger can explode without warning, sending out devastating plumes of swearing and ranting. Disconcertingly calm one minute with no outward sign that they are going to blow, something as minor as a five-minute delay can see the lid blast off. The Krakatoa is secretly admired by other commuters who are too repressed to give vent to their own true feelings, but like to see someone blaze away with both barrels at the powers that be.

The throbbing vein

The throbbing vein is pretty much within the red zone all the time. Even from a distance you can see they're livid, and the slightest setback is going to send them into incandescent rage. Red faced, eyes

→

popping, and with a ready supply of spittle to spray upon anyone they elect to shout at, they often look as if they could use a good drink, or have in fact already had one.

The assassin

Cold and calculating, the assassin gives nothing away. To look at them you would never know that they have seen three buses drive straight past their stop this very morning. But inside they are already planning their revenge, mentally drafting searing emails of complaint, conjuring the Facebook campaigns they will create and the Tweets they will send, all designed to wring out an apology and refund. Don't cross them: the assassin is an implacable enemy. They once waged, and won, a three-year battle with eBay over a faulty George Foreman grill they bought second hand.

The Croydon Bends: An irrational feeling that one is on the wrong train, usually accompanied by a feeling that even if one is on the right train, it won't stop at the right station

Miles Kington

Five things you wish you didn't know about the London Underground

1. Seats on the District, Circle, Northern, Piccadilly, Hammersmith and City, Jubilee and Metropolitan lines are never cleaned. Those on the Bakerloo, Central and Victoria lines only get a shampoo every six months to a year.

2. According to a study carried out by the University of Surrey, passengers on the tube are exposed to five times as much pollution as those in cars.

3. There are around 1,000 bodies buried underneath Aldgate station – it's built over a plague pit from 1665.

4. The tube is home to a distinct breed of biting mosquito called '*moletus*' that thrives underground, and is genetically different to above-ground mozzies.

5. An estimated half-a-million mice live in the tunnels. In 2012, a message on a board in Farringdon station warned that they had begun biting passengers. TfL claimed it was a joke, but who knows …

The rail commuter's Serenity Prayer no.2

God: Grant me the Suppleness of an eel to be able to wriggle onto the packed carriage; the 360-degree Vision of an owl to spot any free seat; and the Strength of a rhino to be able to barge my way off at my stop.

Whenever I travel I like to keep the seat next to me empty. I found a great way to do it. When someone walks down the aisle and says to you, 'Is someone sitting there?' just say, 'No one — except the Lord'

Carol Leifer

Mr Petri Dish

One of the most unpleasant beasts in the
commuter animal kingdom, *Mr Petri Dish* is a
walking, talking, snot-spraying nightmare. Its
persistent sniffing gives it away as a human
incubator of infection. Grown men visibly flinch as
Mr Petri Dish lets out a sneeze, casting a fine film of
mucus over half the carriage. There's nowhere to
hide, as half the people within range grimly resign
themselves to the fact that they'll probably wake
up tomorrow with a stinking cold. British reserve
ensures nothing is said, either. Frankly, you could
board public transport in the UK with bubonic
plague and no one would mention it.

Super-commuters

Some people must really love their job, and are prepared to commute hundreds of miles to get to work. Or they might have a really demanding boss. Either way, super-commuting is on the up, where hopping on a plane to go to work is nothing special. America is the home of the super-commuter, where workers live in one state and fly to another for work. In Houston, Texas, for example, about 15 per cent of the workforce jet in for work from other cities. But the honour of the world's greatest super-commuter probably belongs to a Brit, a police officer with the Met who flew in from New Zealand (that's 12,000 miles each way) for work.

First class →

← Cattle class

What they say and what they mean no.2

Drinks trolley

A small metal cabinet on wheels, akin to that found on an aeroplane, operated by a member of the train company's staff. Conspicuously absent when your journey is so awful that you're desperate to part with £5.50 for a can of warm Heineken, always present when you're trying to snooze in an aisle seat without being clonked every twenty minutes by an inexperienced trolley driver.

Rail replacement bus service

A cruel twist to a journey, in which one inadequate form of transport is replaced by an even worse one. Particularly aggravating is the way that train companies make out they are doing everyone a massive favour by running a bus service, presenting it as a courtesy rather than an indictment of their ability to run a properly functioning railway. Rail replacement bus services also have their own unique mathematical laws, in that any journey made on them always takes more than three times as long as it would have done on the train.

Rush hour

A 'hilariously' named phenomenon that specifically prohibits you from rushing anywhere and is never, ever restricted to one hour. Depending on where you live, it usually occurs from about 7am–10am on a weekday morning, and 4pm–7pm in the evening. Or a little earlier when the schools are let out. And then when everyone's trying to get home from the pub before the transport stops, at around 10.30–11.30pm. Or on a Saturday when everyone decides to go to B&Q at the same time. Or at 11am on a Tuesday when the bus is inexplicably packed.

Strike!

As if having intermittent public transport isn't bad enough, at least once or twice a year a strike will mean there's none at all. Whether it's over holiday, conditions, pay or the wrong type of donuts, it's bound to happen sooner or later. The best thing to do is not to go to work at all of course, but if it can't be avoided, make sure you are ready with your 'competitive commuting' line. For all those that do make it in will be desperate to boast of the lengths they went to get to the office: 'I started walking from Harrow at 1 am.' 'I took an Uber to the park and ride and then a Shetland pony.' 'I had to get a dolphin as far as the Millennium Bridge.'

Johnny Suitcase

There he goes, pushing his way through a crowded station. Not for him the *carrying* of objects, for his bag has wheels! He happily drags it behind him, oblivious to the hapless commuters who, unable to see the little bag in the crowd, tumble sprawling over it, like skittles in *Johnny Suitcase*'s wake.

The posher, more aggressive cousin of *Johnny Suitcase* is of course *Ski Bag Dude*. At five foot long and harder to spot, the bag is invariably being dragged along by someone called Piers who is rushing to get the Heathrow Express and make his flight to Val d'Isère, and couldn't care less what sort of trip hazard he causes on the way.

The most common of all antagonisms arises from a man's taking a seat beside you on the train, a seat to which he is completely entitled

Robert Benchley

☹ Depressing commuter fact no.2

It's bad for your love life

It's hard to be romantic after standing for two hours in cattle class on the way home. The last thing you feel like doing is cooking a nice meal and lighting the candles; what you really want to do is kick off your shoes, slump in a chair and swig neat gin from the bottle in front of *Eastenders*. So it's no surprise to learn that researchers in Sweden found, in a 10-year study, that couples who commuted for more than 45 minutes every day were 40 per cent more likely to divorce.

The Tao of commuting

What can we learn from great thinkers that might help us with the daily grind? Here follows is a collection of wisdom and insight to make it all a bit more bearable. Or at least let you masquerade as a bit of an intellectual. Think and be calm, Grasshopper!

Every calamity is to be overcome by endurance – **Virgil**

A good traveller has no fixed plans, and is not intent on arriving – **Lao Tzu**

The only way of catching a train I ever discovered is to miss the train before – **G.K. Chesterton**

Law of the Alibi: If you tell the boss you were late for work because you had a flat tyre, the very next morning you will have a flat tyre.

Bad is never good until worse happens
– **Danish Proverb**

Sometimes it's necessary to go a long distance out of the way in order to come back a short distance correctly
– **Edward Albee**

You can't wake a person who is pretending to be asleep – **Navajo proverb**

If a man knows not to which port he sails, no wind is favourable – **Seneca**

That which does not kill us makes us stronger – **Nietzsche**

Insanity: doing the same thing over and over again and expecting different results – **Albert Einstein**

Even if you're foreign
or have children

Stand on the damn right

Working from home

Working from home! Living the dream! Avoiding the commute altogether! Winning!

This is what you might think when you convince your boss that you'd be so much more productive if only you didn't have to spend an hour and a half trying to get to the office very day. And it's true, for a while. You roll out of bed later, and listen to the traffic bulletins on the radio, with the reports of strikes, delays and jams, as you whistle a happy tune and make yourself an elaborate breakfast.

But what all homeworkers eventually discover is that having to turn up to the office does at least force you to make some sort of effort to conform to the rules of normal society. For one thing, it means you have to get dressed, as travelling to work in pyjamas is considered beyond the pale. Unless you work for *Vogue*, in which case it is very much on point. Plus, of course, commuting takes you away from the telly and fridge, the evil twin sirens that call out constantly to the tormented homeworker.

The cyclist's highway code

Bike commuting is getting more and more popular, and with so many new cyclists hitting the road some ground rules are needed to keep things moving.

1. Red lights *are* for stopping at. Fact! Who knew that this was an actual thing?

2. Headphones are a must. A soundtrack of hard techno can help you find a good pedalling rhythm and power you along. Also, it drowns out abuse from white van drivers.

3. Treat pedestrians as dumb sheep. They just wander anywhere, so make sure you have their attention by angrily bellowing at them if they have the temerity to walk in the bike lane.

4. Use hand signals to let other road users know your intentions. Two of the most useful are the raised middle finger, and the shaking fist that is the universal sign for 'wanker'.

5.   Remember, drivers are generally embittered and envious of your freedom and taut glutes. That is why they are trying to knock you off, not because you insist on riding at 5mph in the middle of the road.

6.   Cyclists are cool. Remember to give your work colleagues a fashion treat when you get to work by sashaying through the office in your lycra leotard. Hey, you don't need to change until after at least your third meeting of the day!

7.   Don't be a wet weather martyr. If it's raining, just bring your bike onto the train. No one minds!

Underground codes

It's one of the many weird quirks of the British,
that if the tube is delayed due to someone having
jumped in front of a train, the announcement will
go something like this: 'this train is delayed due
to a person on the tracks'. If, however, there is
an incident involving some wee, or a bit of sick,
say, TfL's announcers go all coy. Listen out for
the following codes used over the PA system on
London Underground to alert a cleaning team to a
particular situation:

Code 1: Blood

Code 2: Urine/faeces

Code 3: Vomit

Code 4: Spillage

Code 5: Broken glass

Code 6: Litter

Code 7 is used for anything not fitting these
categories (the mind boggles) and 'Inspector Sands'
heard over the loudspeaker means a fire alarm has
gone off, and staff have two minutes to get to the
control room to deactivate it, or the station will
be evacuated.

Seat remorse (n.)

Seat remorse arises from two possible sources. There is something wrong with the seat itself. Or there is something wrong with the occupants of the adjacent seats. Neither is good. Whether it's a seat that is inexplicably wet and/or smelly, to a neighbour who appears to have forgotten their trousers, one question immediately presents itself: should I face the embarrassment and get back up? Or should I tough it out and stay, pretending I'm not bothered and don't regret sitting here at all.

Guerilla commuting

When you've really had enough, it's tempting to go a bit rogue. You're an old hand at this commuting business, and it's time for the rookies to stand aside …

- Had enough of idiots who insist on wearing their backpacks on public transport, sideswiping everyone when they suddenly turn 180 degrees? Make your own set of 'I'm a bag wanker' stickers, which you can gently affix to their rucksack without them knowing.

- Carry a newspaper to foil the aisle-seat hogger. This is the person who sits on the outside seat in the belief that no one will try to get by them to the empty one by the window. Simply toss your paper across them to the vacant spot, putting them instantly in checkmate. Now they can't slide across – that's your seat now – and they're going to have to stand up to let you in.

- Follow your train or bus company on Twitter. As soon as there's a problem, start tweeting them. It might not make the trains run on time, but you'll be able to keep up a steady stream of sarcastic criticism that will make you feel so much better. If you can shoehorn in pictures of a crammed carriage full of weeping children, even better. Doesn't matter if it's not your train – it's all about *your* truth, right?

- Fed up with your elbow being pushed off the armrest by the big bloke in the next seat? Then unleash your inner absent-minded professor and get some sticky elbow patches for your jacket. This extra grip means that you won't endure the train-riding equivalent of sand being kicked in your face by bigger boys.

Always take the weather

Weather is something we have no shortage of on these little islands. And yet it always seems to take our transport network by surprise …

Even just the lightest sprinkling of rain seems to make everyone drive like an idiot

It's a well-known fact that in heavy rain all buses mysteriously vanish, leading many people to believe they are water soluble.

It may be a glorious day above ground, but the tube has turned into a fiery furnace and even the toughest commuters are swooning like Victorian maidens.

Two centimetres of snow is enough to bring apocalyptic chaos to all transport in Great Britain. Even, mysteriously, to Glasgow's subway and London's Victoria line – both of which are entirely underground.

A breezy autumn is guaranteed to bring rail chaos with fallen trees, or, everyone's favourite rail company excuse – leaves on the line! Yes, that old chestnut. (Probably some of them on the line too.)

Thunderstorms and resulting flash floods are terrible news for commuters, but great news for newspapers, who can fill their pages with photos of firemen giving piggybacks to little old ladies and knock off early for the day.

The Statue

An increasingly common sighting, this creature is
a distant cousin of the head-in-sand ostrich. With
eyes fixed on its book or phone and headphones
clamped on, this commuter has shut out the
outside world. Little old lady with walking stick
struggles on to the tube needing to sit down?
Forget it! *The Statue* is wedged into its seat (usually
the one with the 'please give up this seat' sign) and
is deaf to all appeals to decency.

Complaint template no.3

Dear _____

I consider myself a normal guy, who enjoys recreational activities as much as the next person. I am, for example, a keen golfer, and enjoy indoor pastimes too, such as Monopoly and Snap. What I am trying to convey is that I usually enjoy fun and games. However, I must write to tell you that I do not find the games that your bus drivers are playing any fun at all. Every day I wait to see if the bus will stop. If it does, will the driver open the doors, or simply pull away again? And if I do manage to get on board, will he acknowledge my bus stop, even though I have RUNG THE BELL 10 TIMES? I might enjoy this game more if I understood any of the rules and knew what to expect. Perhaps you would be kind enough to send me instructions about how to use your bus service, as I am obviously doing it wrong in some way! I will share this with my fellow would-be passengers as they don't have a clue, either.

With no good wishes, etc

Cycling to work

For some people, there comes a day when they can't face the commute any more, continually suffering as a plaything of the merciless train and

Pros
You can be smug in the knowledge that you are doing your bit for the planet
Is there anything nicer than jumping on your bike first thing on a lovely sunny morning?
The freedom to go when and where you want to go; not to rely on the capriciousness of bus routes or train timetables
Just don your bike gear, grab your backpack and go!
A great way to build exercise into your routine – getting your heart rate up twice a day means you can ditch the gym membership!
You can pedal to work happy in the thought of all that money saved from the hands of rail companies

bus companies. It is at this point that they become a herb farmer in rural Wales, or they decide to join the cycling set and bike into work. So what are the pros and cons?

Cons
The planet does not seem to be doing its bit for you, as you cough and splutter in clouds of traffic fumes
Oh, it's raining
Trying to wrestle your bike onto the 21.32 train home after five pints at an impromptu pub trip
On opening your backpack at work you realise your trousers are still hanging over the chair in your bedroom. Today you will be going to meetings dressed in lycra
Your heart rate soars every time an oblivious pedestrian steps out almost under your bike wheels – as does your blood pressure when the third taxi driver of the morning cuts you up
Showering at work is always going to feel a bit weird, isn't it? I mean, you're naked. At work

Be mindful
of the gap

You may think that commuting and inner peace
are mutually incompatible. Wrong! With the help
of these simple mindfulness techniques, you can
achieve the unperturbable calm of the Dalai Lama.
Although, let's face it, he's never had to face the
8.02 to Swindon on a rainy Monday morning.

- Mindfulness is about relaxing the physical
  body, so the spirit may roam freely. So sit down
  and spread out your limbs. Can't get a seat or
  move your limbs more than a few millimetres?
  Oh dear. Move to next step.

- Mindfulness means acceptance, and that
  includes accepting that you can't sit down.
  Reflect on how lucky you are to be able to
  simply stand with your fellow man, packed
  together in silent grateful communion.

- Be thankful along your journey. Thank the
  doors of the train for letting you off. Thank the
  escalator for sparing you the effort of climbing
  stairs. Thank the tourist who is standing on
  the wrong side of the escalator for forcing you

to slow down and providing you a moment to calmly reflect on the big meeting you are already late for.

- Appreciate the natural beauty around you. Study your fellow commuters and really take time to look at the myriad wonders of the human body you never noticed before. Isn't it amazing how many different pallid shades of grey skin can look? And who knew ear hair grew in such abundant curly clumps?

- Breathe deeply, getting the air right down deep into your lungs to centre yourself and build spiritual energy. The particles of body odour, fast food and smelly breath you inhale will nourish your inner wellbeing.

- Try to let go of material concerns, and focus on the positives. Instead of bitterly reflecting on the price of your season ticket when the train is delayed again, think of the lovely morning that the train driver has had, rolling out of bed late and sauntering to the station before starting his working day. Be glad that someone is having a good day, and the universe may grant you one, too. Maybe.

The Bagbuddy

Characterised by a bustling gait and aura of entitlement, this creature is a loner. Found on all types of public transport, *The Bagbuddy* likes two seats. One for it, one for its bag. Who cares if people have to stand? It's important that its rucksack – containing an empty water bottle and yesterday's *Metro* – rides in state alongside. It can be fun watching it get all huffy when asked to move its bag, which it regards as a terrible infringement of its human rights.

A close relation to *The Bagbuddy* is *The Plane-Plonker* who brings an in appropriately massive case onto the plane and then takes up all the overhead locker space with it. One of the few highlights of budget airline autocracy is seeing it thwarted at the boarding gate when the cabin crew tell it the bag is too big and has to go in the hold.

The tactical hangback (n.)

The homing instinct is strong in the commuter. Some people will literally do anything to make their train or bus home, sprinting out mid-meeting to get there in time if that's what it takes. Career prospects be damned; the 17.09 to Kettering is what matters. The result is that all the same can't-be-late-me-first-out-of-my-way types want to rush on to the first train back. A carriage full of punctilious obsessives is a grim place to be, given that they are the kind of joyless mob as likely to offer you their seat as they are to leave their underpants unironed.

What they don't realise though, is that although the tortoise commuter might not beat the hare home, they have a much more pleasant journey. The seasoned commuter knows the first train that will be relatively free of such zealots and enjoys the more humane conditions.

How annoying are you?

1. **You like listen to music on your commute. Do you?**

a) Have a huge pair of Apollo 11 spaceman-type headphones that shut out the world
b) Use the ear buds that came with your phone. They do a job
c) Don't bother with headphones and just play music direct from your phone
d) Carry a huge beatbox to blast out tunes, because everyone likes some hip hop in the morning, right?

Answer: a) You are a considerate traveller, although a tiny bit annoying if someone has to tap you on the shoulder to tell you you're standing on their foot. b) Not too bad, although the tinny beat escaping from your ears can quickly get old for other passengers. c) You are annoying, full stop. Get some headphones, or get off the bus. d) You have time travelled from 1983 and should return there quickly.

2. **You are going on a business trip and have a small suitcase with you. Do you?**

a) Park it in the designated luggage spot and leave it there

b)   Stuff it into any available space you can find
     and then go off to find a seat
c)   Insist on keeping it next to you at all times
d)   Pile your luggage on top of someone else's

Answers: a) Well done. Obedient people like you keep the whole show on the road. b) At least you're making an effort, but you run the risk of making everyone else anxious about the unattended package dumped by the door. c) What's so crucial about your change of pants that you can't let your bag out of your sight? Stop being a pain and put it in the luggage rack. d) You have committed a terrible offence. Touching another man's bag is like touching his wife: a complete no-no unless he's given permission.

3.   You bring some reading material for the journey. Is this?

a)   A Kindle or slim paperback
b)   A broadsheet newspaper
c)   A set of huge leatherbound volumes
d)   A large Ordnance Survey fold-out map

Answers: a) Your sensible choice marks you out as a person of consideration and refinement. You're probably reading some high-end literature. Or Jackie Collins. No one can tell on a Kindle. b) Impractical, a little selfish and unnecessary. We know you're a high-powered businessman, from the red socks and aura of entitlement. You don't need to unfurl the FT as well. c) This is not the time or place to start on the complete works of Darwin. You have mistaken the 8.20 to Paddington for a library. d) You are a tourist. You are lost. In recognition of this you will be allowed exactly 35 seconds to put your map away and stand quietly like everyone else, before people start glaring at you and tutting.

Score:
a = 1 point, b = 2 points, c = 3 points, d = 4 points

4 points and below. You are a model commuter. Considerate and polite, you are the ideal type. Someone could commute next to you for 15 years and never notice you.

6–7 points. Not bad, but you need to watch out. Some of your personal preferences might be raising the odd hackle. Not that anyone will ever say anything to you, of course. This is Britain.

8–10 points. You are annoying, the kind of person people change carriages to get away from. Don't expect anyone to help you if you one day fail to mind the gap.

11 points and above. You are the type of person people talk about in the office when they arrive at work '*You'll never believe what this bloke was doing on the train this morning*'. This complete disregard for conventions and other people would be almost admirable if it wasn't so irritating.

You know, somebody actually complimented me on my driving today. They left a little note on the windscreen, it said 'Parking Fine'

Tommy Cooper

And now for the traffic and travel ... from history

The first recorded British traffic jam was in AD43. Approximately ten minutes after the Romans finished the very first road, the Britons immediately decided to use it all at exactly the same time, creating the first ever rush hour. Here are some more traffic reports discovered by historians.

AD 500 (approx) – Jousting has broken on on the Arthurian Way northbound to Camelot, creating severe delays. Reports suggest traffic is backed up to Stonehenge.

1066 – Major disruption in the Hastings area due to sudden large number of French drivers on the wrong side of road. There are diversions in place – just look out for the arrows.

1297 – A monk has shed a sandal on the pilgrimage road to Canterbury, causing slow moving traffic. On the same stretch an apparition of the Blessed Lady outside Faversham is also causing tailbacks.

Travellers are advised to pray to their favourite saint to clear the hold-ups.

1538 – Long delays in the Hampton Court area today, as Henry VIII and courtiers are out hunting for a new wife. Advice is to avoid the area if you can, especially if you are female, unmarried and enjoy keeping your head on your neck.

1701 – Reports of highwayman activity on the King's Highway in the woods just outside York. All vehicles being made to wait in a queue for operation 'Stand and Deliver'. Hold-ups are expected.

1798 – A number of upper-class gentlemen sporting pistols and long swords, standing twenty paces apart are causing tailbacks just outside the bounds of London. Motorists are advised to avoid the duel carriageway.

2017 – It's being reported that the long delays around the Westminster area today are being caused by a large number of sudden U-turns.

About the Author

Commuting has occupied a large part of Jonathan Swan's life. An ill-fated business trip saw him trapped going round and round on the Circle Line from 1992–94; he has also failed to mind the gap on at least three occasions. As a result he nowadays mostly stays at home.